the

PREGNANT
BRIDE'S GUIDE

TO A STRESS-FREE WEDDING

ABOUT THE SERIES

Something Different Wedding Guides are comprehensive guides, created for the couple who value tradition but do not want to being either constrained or intimidated by it. Each guide addresses a contemporary issue in wedding planning.

DISCLAIMER

Although Jennifer Cram has taken every care in preparing and writing this book, she accepts no liability for any errors, omissions, misuse, or misunderstanding on the part of any person who uses it. Reliance on the material in this book shall be at your sole risk. The author specifically disclaims any implied warranty of fitness for any particular purpose and accepts no responsibility for any damage, injury, or loss occasioned to any person as a result of relying on any material included, omitted, or implied.

the

PREGNANT BRIDE'S GUIDE

TO A STRESS-FREE WEDDING

JENNIFER CRAM
Authorized Marriage Celebrant

Something Different Wedding Guides

Something Old
Something New
Something Borrowed
Something Blue
Something Different

CONTENTS

1 INTRODUCTION

When you announce that you're getting married it seems that everyone you know has something to say, and generally speaking they feel entitled to tell you how you must do it, and to feel offended if you don't comply with their idea of what a proper wedding is.

The days when a rushed and secret wedding was the only option for the pregnant bride have, thankfully, long gone. Today most people are more relaxed about what used to be referred to as "anticipating the wedding" However, despite huge improvements in social mores, when you're a pregnant bride you will in all likelihood have to deal with some less positive expectations and remarks or advice aimed at convincing you to tone down your plans for your wedding, change the color of your wedding dress, or omit the veil.

But, if you focus on the big picture, embrace the special joy (and glow) of being a pregnant bride, accommodate your pregnancy to ensure that you are comfortable on the day, and use the techniques in this book to manage your budget, wedding arrangements, and the expectations of others, you'll have a fantastic day and be in a good position to welcome your new addition to the family when the time comes.

About half of wedding planning involves making decisions. The other half consists of emotionally digesting societal expectations, generational expectations, and the often very strangely condescending and pushy attitude of vendors/wedding service providers who are meant to be offering you a service. Being prepared for that helps enormously in enabling you to stick to your guns about what you want for your wedding.

The major sources of wedding stress tend to be:

- Money

- Unrealistic expectations of perfection

- Power struggles resulting from the expectations of family and friends

- Vendors who become incredibly hyperactive when trying to sell you very expensive ideas – and who pounce and push if you show the slightest hesitation

- Incorrect assumptions regarding what is included in booked services.

- Wedding pranks

- The weather

For the pregnant bride, the physical and emotional changes you are experiencing and the expectations of others in relation to your impending motherhood are added to this already long list.

I hope you will find this book a useful aid to keeping your wedding as stress-free (and glitch-free) as possible. And that you have a fabulous day.

2 THE WEDDING DECISION MAKING PROCESS ...

... and how the White Wedding Industry uses this to manipulate you into Spending, Spending, and Spending even more.

There is a hierarchy of decision making that applies to weddings

- Emotional, based on fear and competitiveness

- Instinctive, based on gut feelings

- Intellectual based on an assessment of practicality.

The wedding industry counts on pushing you into making emotional decisions. Vendors may use methods such as preying on a natural fear of being judged by your family and friends and found wanting, appealing to your competitive side, or creating an impression of scarcity and thus they prey on your fear of missing out if you don't sign up then and there.

The wedding industry tolerates instinctive decisions (when you just go with your gut feeling) but absolutely abhors intellectual ones for a very simple reason.

How much money you will spend will reduce at each stage in the decision-making process.

If you make an emotional decision, you will spend most because you won't be thinking critically about the decision. If you make an instinctive decision, you will spend slightly less because there will be some filtering going on, based on past experience and other factors. If you make an intellectual decision you will spend even less because you will be weighing up whether the decision is a good one for you.

So take the time to make sure you work through all three stages for every wedding-related decision. Acknowledge your emotions, pay attention to your gut feelings, and then make an intellectual decision taking into account all the facts.

Another thing worth considering is that the white wedding industry is very much about targeting the way we buy with our eyes. That's why it is mostly about stuff - things that can be photographed. But this approach, while it certainly increases the bottom line profit for most wedding-related businesses, ignores the fact that the content of your ceremony can only be "bought" with the heart. Memories are made with the heart, and a wonderful ceremony and celebration is really about your relationship with family and friends. Focusing on feelings is what will make your wedding memorable.

And please remember

Guilt and Shame do not have to be invited to your wedding.

Regardless of whether you are pregnant or not, you are entitled to have the wedding you want, and not feel the least bit guilty about doing just that.

3 BUILD YOUR WEDDING BUDGET FROM THE BOTTOM UP

Money is a huge source of wedding stress. However, the good news is that, regardless of the message the white wedding industry conveys, you **can** have a wonderful, memorable wedding without starting your marriage completely broke or in debt.

Bridal magazines and websites generally provide a formula about how to divide up your budget, for example 50% for reception, and give the impression that this is some sort of non-negotiable rule. The formula sort-of works for the reception if you've got a large budget but it does not work for a smaller budget.

So forget about the Budget Formula and stop thinking about how much money you have, your credit card limit, or how much you can borrow. Instead, start thinking of your wedding budget as $0.00, an amount you want to go over as little as possible. You may have a dollar amount in your head, but definitely don't tell anyone else what it is because that number is usually then perceived to be the minimum amount you *wish* to spend, rather than the maximum amount you *cannot* exceed.

Using the template below as a guide, list all those things you want and need:

Our Wedding Budget Priorities

MUST HAVE—the MARRIAGE (Cost $ ....)
1. Marriage Licence (where required)
2. Making it Legal (the Marriage Ceremony)
3. Official Marriage Certificate / Copy of Licence

WANT AND POSSIBLY NEED—the WEDDING
Budget $0.00
Intention: To go as little over budget as possible

FIXED COSTS (i.e. not affected by the number of guests)	VARIABLE COSTS (i.e. directly affected by the number of guests)
CEREMONY VENUE HIRE	RECEPTION FOOD
RINGS	RECEPTION DRINKS
WEDDING DRESS	RECEPTION MUSIC
PHOTOGRAPHER	TABLE DECORATION
TRANSPORT (for bridal party)	FAVORS
etc	etc

Figure 1: Budget Template

Once you have listed everything you can think of, rearrange your list in order of priority, putting those most important to you at the top of the list

Now start costing each item on the list.

Draw a line when you get to the amount you would feel comfortable spending.

Everything above the line now fits into your actual budget, but your work isn't done. This is the point where tips about how to save on individual items come into their own.

Start thinking outside the box about how you will achieve these items for the least cost (thereby reducing your total cost), without compromising your priorities and keep telling yourself that the wedding industry is keen to make you overspend your budget - most couples overspend by at least 20%.

But also don't forget the old mantra *You get what you pay for.* Sometimes cheap at the outset turns out more expensive in the long run. Don't compromise on quality for the things that mean most to you.

Reality Check
Variable costs will usually be quoted on a per person basis. Make sure you note the per-person **and** the total for each item on your budget sheet. On a per guest basis, the more guests you have the higher your variable costs. Your fixed costs will always be quoted as total cost per item (for example the total cost of the dress).

For a reality check where appropriate divide each of the fixed costs by the number of guests, such as the wedding decorations, ceremony venue hire, etc. See how this works in the following example:

If it costs $300 to hire the ceremony venue
and you have 100 guests
that's $3 per guest.

If you have 10 guests, it is $30 per guest.

4 GUARD YOUR IDENTITY

In all the excitement (and stress) of planning your wedding and trying to get the biggest bang for your budget, it is understandable that one of the biggest risks to your security is not exactly on your radar. Brides are prime targets for those looking to rip you off by stealing your credit details and even your identity.

Beware of websites that offer you freebies in return for contact information where they want more than just your first name, an email address and some minimal information about date of wedding and broad geographical location of your venue.

Be careful about what information you give to online discount suppliers of wedding dresses and other items. Just because a website looks like it is a local one, doesn't necessarily mean it is. Providing credit card and other personal details can give scam sites all the data they need to do your finances and/or credit rating some serious damage.

Nobody, apart from your officiant and those responsible for the legal registration of your marriage, has a legitimate reason for asking for your date of birth.

Do not, whatever you do, post a photograph of your marriage license or marriage certificate on the web, on your Face Book page, or on any other social media or photo-sharing site. It is all very exciting to receive these documents, but they include identifying information including your mother's maiden name (often used as a security question by banks) your address, and your occupation. Having access to any or all of those things is a great help to identity thieves, who are dab hands at collecting related bits of information to build up a more complete picture. Also, make sure your official photographer doesn't take or post photographs with signatures visible.

Though using PayPal will protect your bank and credit card information don't be lulled into a false sense of security by paying via PayPal. Unless you can be sure that you will be able to open a dispute and request a refund within 60 days, PayPal's refund policy won't reimburse you. If you buy a wedding dress online from overseas typically delivery time is much longer than that.

5 EMBRACE BEING A PREGNANT BRIDE

Marriage is a cause for celebration. And so is pregnancy. Being pregnant gives you all the more reason to celebrate marrying the love of your life.

Yes, being pregnant means that you need to consider a variety of things that don't need to be on the radar for a bride who is not pregnant, but these variables can prompt you to think outside the box, enabling you to create an extra-special experience for everyone present.

Deal with the white dress issue straight away.

While an idea developed in Victorian times that only the virgin bride should wear white, this was a later moral overlay given to a decision that Queen Victoria made to wear a white wedding gown was merely a fashion choice. Way back then, whatever the Queen did became a non-negotiable "rule" for the upper classes, whose customs and fashions were then invariably adopted by the middle classes and viewed as a rigid code of behavior.

Today we have come full circle and most people view the white wedding dress as a traditional fashion choice and do not attach any emotional baggage to it.

But equally so, you should not feel you have to wear white to make a point. You can wear any color you choose without feeling you are conveying a message that you are no longer entitled to wear white.

Nor do you have to choose a wedding dress that conceals your baby bump. Again, it is a matter of choice. Flaunt it if you wish. Discreetly conceal it if you prefer.

6 MANAGE THE EXPECTATIONS OF OTHERS

Family and friends always have expectations and strong opinions when it comes to weddings. When the bride is pregnant the intensity of these tends to ramp up, particularly with older women who were themselves coerced into marrying quickly and quietly, and to feel ashamed about being pregnant on their wedding day. They may resent that you are proudly showing off your bump and that society generally accepts that pregnancy need not compromise anyone's plans for the wedding of their dreams.

It may sound harsh, but, in my experience, the best way to manage the expectations of family and friends and to limit the amount of pressure they may put on you to marry in their preferred way (usually expressed using terms such as *must, traditional, proper etiquette, the way it is always done* and similar guilt inducing justifications) is to limit the power you give others.

The best way to do this is to limit how much you share. If you don't think aloud in their presence, don't ask their opinion, don't seek their advice, and don't discuss your ideas you will be free to make a list of those things you know you *definitely do not want* to include in your wedding and stick to it.

And you will also be free to

- Take a wiser, more modern 21st century approach to your wedding

- Do only what feels right for both of you in the context of your relationship

- Ignore traditions that are in reality just disguised superstitions

- Eliminate gender stereotypes that perpetuate the notion of the bride being a second class citizen on her way to becoming the possession of her husband

- Acknowledge the child you're expecting in the ceremony

- Ask for and accept help for specific tasks (delegate anything and everything except the decision-making)

- Stand firm on what you will and will not tolerate for your wedding – if outdated wedding pranks leave you cold you should say so in no uncertain terms.

- Refuse to allow anyone who is generously paying for all or part of your wedding to hold you to ransom over it..

However, there are some things that are critical to share both early and often:

- When and where the ceremony and the reception will be held

- Start and end times for both the ceremony and the reception

- How to get there and how long it will take to do so - and if the ceremony and the reception are being held in different places, the best route between the two.

- Details about parking, access, and anything unusual about the venue

- If a religious ceremony, any dress restrictions or expectations

- Venue restrictions on confetti, rice, rose petals etc. and how much you will be charged or fined for clean-up if guests ignore the restrictions.

- Your wishes about guests taking photographs or video footage during the ceremony, and your wishes regarding what they share on social media.

7 CHECK WITH YOUR CHURCH

If you are planning to marry in a religious ceremony, you may find that the wider social acceptance of a pregnant bride might not be reflected in the response of your church or individual member of the clergy to your pregnancy.

Some will not accept a pregnant bride, but many will. However, these latter may expect you to have a small, low-key wedding ceremony.

It is best to ascertain whether your first choice of church is viable, and whether you are comfortable with any compromises you may be expected to make.

If it doesn't work out, keep asking around.

8 ACCOMMODATE YOUR PREGNANCY

If you're just starting to plan your wedding you will be able to take your needs into account from the get-go. If, however, your planning is in train and you've just discovered that you are pregnant, it would be wise to make some adjustments to your plans.

As your pregnancy progresses, everyday activities such as sitting and standing for lengthy periods of times can become uncomfortable. Fluid can build up in your legs and feet when you are motionless for more than 15 minutes. You will also tire more quickly or start to feel light-headed, particularly when standing

Plan to manage fatigue

Consider how much time each part of your day will take - the ceremony, photography sessions, the cocktail hour, the speeches, the reception and so on - and look for ways you can pare down the time needed for each and how you can make adjustments to allow you to be comfortable.

Some strategies you can use are:
- Arrange for chairs to be placed in strategic places for you to sit when needed.

- In consultation with your officiant, redesign your ceremony space. Plan to sit for part or all of the ceremony, but make sure that the seating you choose allows your guests to see you. High bar stools, a sofa or two chairs on a dais, or a simple bench will all serve.

- Have an extra chair placed at each table at your reception so that you can move around and interact with your guests but not need to stand for any length of time.

- Keep your personal vows short. It takes more effort to distil your thoughts into fewer words, but it is worth the effort, not only as a fatigue-management strategy but also because doing so increases the impact of your promises, makes them more powerful.

- Ensure your wedding dress is comfortable, that your undergarments are not restricting, and that you can make a quick toilet stop without involving an army of helpers.

- Wear comfortable flat shoes. They won't show under your dress, and they will be less tiring than heels. You will also be less likely to overbalance, stumble, or fall.

- Consider wearing support hose. They will help control swelling in your feet and lower legs, reduce leg ache, and won't show under your dress.

- Ensure that your reception venue has temperature control. There is nothing more tiring than being over-heated for lengthy periods.

- Make sure that you have easy access to plenty of water and to bathrooms.

Your Wedding Dress

Gone are the days when maternity clothes featured little girl features like peter pan collars and made you look like a frump with a bump. Today maternity clothes are every bit as stylish and gorgeous as regular clothes, and bridal stores cater for the pregnant bride, carrying a range of designs to suit every stage of pregnancy. However, they tend not to advertise that they do so because, in the wider scheme of things, they do not view it as a selling point.

No one can accurately predict how much your body will change or how you will carry during your pregnancy, so you will have different issues to deal with compared with the bride who is boot-camp obsessed with being thinner than normal on the day.

If this isn't your first pregnancy don't assume that your body will change in the same way as before. It probably won't as each pregnancy is unique.

If you are marrying during the first trimester of your pregnancy you will have more style options to choose from and fewer complications regarding fit. If you are marrying in your second or third trimester, sizing is absolutely key to achieving the wow factor. So the first thing to consider and tell the consultant in the bridal store is how many weeks pregnant you will be on your wedding day. A few weeks can make a big difference. Also make sure you tell the consultant what your normal pattern of weight fluctuation is.

Bridal stores use bust measurements to help predict what size you will be on your wedding day. Your current bust measure allows them to see where you fall on a particular designer's size chart. They then add one inch for each month until your wedding (so, for example, if your wedding is in 4 months they will add 4 inches to your current bust measure to see where you will fall on the size chart) plus an extra inch as a failsafe.

The next major decision is style. You will need to tell the consultant whether you are happy to show off your baby bump or would prefer to be more discreet about it. A snug fit, such as a mermaid or trumpet style dress, will enhance your curves and give you a more dramatic look but will need expert alteration right at the last minute to ensure a perfect fit. An empire line dress with a flowing skirt made of chiffon, georgette or organza will downplay the bump, as will more elaborate decoration at the top of the bodice. Accentuating the shoulders and bust will draw the eye away from your bump. A vee-neck will also give the impression of a more elongated body than a strapless gown.

Other suitable dress styles are princess line and A line, both of which skim the waist and hips rather than emphasize them. Avoid styles that are constricting, such as those with a tightly laced bodice.

Your Shoes

Five inch heels are not a good choice for someone with an altered center of gravity and aching, swollen feet and ankles. Find some cute and comfortable flats. Ensure that your shoes will fit on the day (as your pregnancy progresses it is highly likely that you shoe size will increase) by not shopping for shoes too far ahead and by seriously considering buying shoes a half size larger than you usually wear together with some inserts just in case they are a little loose on the day.

Your Veil

Forget about any nonsense that a wedding veil should not be worn by a pregnant bride. If you want to wear one, go ahead. But take extra care to choose a style that both coordinates with your dress and works with your bump.

Your Wedding Ring

Fingers commonly swell during pregnancy. If you choose a ring that is too small you will risk cutting off the circulation in your finger if you manage to get it on your finger on the day. There is not much that is less edifying in a wedding ceremony than watching a mighty struggle to force the ring on.

A jeweler can stretch a plain metal wedding ring in order to enlarge it, but making a ring smaller involves cutting a piece out of it and welding it together again. Neither option works with an engraved ring or one set with diamonds. And wearing a larger ring once your finger has returned to normal is not to be advised. Although your engagement ring would stop your wedding ring falling off your finger, a ring that is overly loose that could cause wear to your more-valuable engagement ring.

A simple solution is to use an inexpensive substitute ring the ceremony and wear that ring until after the baby is born.

If it is important to you, you could bring the 'real' ring to the wedding ceremony together with your substitute ring and have your priest or pastor bless it, together with the substitute ring.

If you're including a warming of the rings ritual in your ceremony, pass both the real ring and the substitute ring round the guests so you have their blessing on both rings.

Your Flowers

Pregnancy may increase your sensitivity to fragrances, and odors that previously did not bother you may become distressing. It would be wise to steer clear of highly perfumed flowers both for bouquets and buttonholes, as well as for ceremony and reception decorations

Roses sourced from a florist are usually a good choice as they have been developed to improve their longevity as cut flowers. This generally means they have little or no fragrance. Orchids, which have no fragrance, are another excellent choice.

There are also many high-quality artificial flowers on the market, or you can opt to carry a fan (excellent choice in warmer weather) instead of a bouquet.

You may also need to ask your bridal party to skip the

perfume, aftershave, or cologne.

Your Menu

One of the first pieces of advice your doctor will give you will be to avoid certain foods, including certain types of seafood, raw fish, and soft cheeses, all of which are frequently included in finger foods passed during cocktail hour.

Other risky foods are undercooked meats, and mayonnaise or hollandaise sauces made with eggs.

Ensuring that you are not exposed to any food-related risk on your wedding day isn't selfish, it is sensible.

Examine the menus offered by caterers, ask about the ingredients used and how they are prepared, and request that pregnancy-friendly foods are substituted for those your doctor advises you should avoid.

Make sure that plenty of non-alcoholic drinks are available. A signature mocktail, celebrating your baby as well as your marriage, would encourage your guests to share a drink with you as well as hitting the *real* bar. You could even use a signature mocktail to announce the gender of your baby.

.

9 INCLUDE THE BABY IN YOUR MARRIAGE CEREMONY

If your pregnancy is public information you may wish to include your unborn baby in the ceremony in order to acknowledge and celebrate that you are marrying as a family, not just as a couple. Giving the baby a little attention amplifies the joy - but don't go overboard. It is your wedding day, not a baby shower.

Discuss your wish to include references to the baby in the ceremony with your officiant. Some officiants are more than happy to do this. Others may be more reluctant.

Some options are:

- Ask your officiant to include mention of your baby in his/her welcome at the beginning of the ceremony, for example:

    Today we have gathered together to celebrate _____ and _____'s commitment to one another and to the baby they're looking forward to welcoming into their home.

- Include the lighting of a third, smaller candle, in the Unity Candle ritual, so that when you light the Unity

Candle you are using three flames instead of the usual two. Ask your officiant to include mention of the significance of the third flame as you and your spouse use your individual candles to light the candle representing the baby together, and then use all three candles to light the Unity Candle.

- Choose a family oriented reading and craft an appropriate introduction to the reading.

- Make your vows holding hands, but with your hands on your bump

- Include your baby in your vows. This could be as simple as adding, *and the child we are expecting* or similar words. For example:

> *I promise to love, encourage, and support you*
> *and the child we so eagerly await*
> *as long as I live.*

- Alternatively, include your baby in your ring vows. For example:

> *With this ring I give you my heart*
> *and my commitment to love, honor,*
> *and protect you, the child I/you carry,*
> *and any children who may follow*
> *always.*

- Ask your officiant to include a blessing for your unborn child in the ceremony. For example:

> *The commitment _____ and _____*
> *are making today is to create a home*
> *that is a secure and happy place*
> *for all who live in it.*
> *May their child be blessed with a life*
> *and a home of abundant love, laughter, joy*
> *and quiet contentment.*

- Ask your officiant to include the baby when pronouncing you husband and wife, for example, by pronouncing you *husband, wife, and family*

- Include the baby in wordless expressions of affection. For example, after you exchange your first kiss as husband and wife, each kiss your fingers and gently place your hand on your bump.

10 TRADITIONS AND SUPERSTITIONS

Most wedding traditions have their basis in superstition – what people believe must be done or observed to avoid bad luck. For thousands of years the focus of marriage was procreation, so it stands to reason that many, if not most, traditions and superstitions are about ensuring fertility, and therefore they reinforce the idea that marriage is about procreation rather than the love and support we now look forward to as an essential part of marriage.

This means the pregnant bride is off the hook! Feel free to ignore any and all traditions – particularly the following:

- **Involving small children in the ceremony**
  Flower girls, page boys and ring bearers are supposed to ensure fertility for the couple. In some cultures they also have a small child roll around on the marital bed.

- **Spending money on expensive fresh flowers**
  Carrying a bouquet, decorating with fresh flowers, and having rose petals scattered in your path are ancient customs to ensure fertility. Flowers are symbols of fertility. Many include parts with distinct similarities to both male and female genitalia. Go figure.

- **Throwing rice**
  Tossing rice over the couple was to ensure both fertility and prosperity, a belief that makes sense when you consider that the perceived value of a wife depended on her capacity to bear children who could help produce food for the family, and look after their parents in old age. In agricultural communities poor harvests could result in a drop in the birth rate, hence the association of tossing grains and ensuring fertility.

- **Having a cake, and cutting it**
  The wedding cake is a fertility symbol with a long history. In Ancient Rome a pretty stodgy, bread-like cake made from multiple grains was broken over the bride's head to ensure her fertility. Cutting the cake (with the groom's hand over the bride's on the handle of the knife) has added Freudian symbolism to this intimate ritual.

Regardless of anything anyone might say to you, you've proven your fertility, so most of the traditions based on fertility magic are redundant. Moreover, nothing can influence the outcome of your wedding unless you are obsessive about superstition, in which case the superstition will take over and dominate everything.

In the hundreds and hundreds and hundreds of weddings I have officiated I've never once had any of the following happen:

- the marriage fell apart because the groom saw the bride's dress before the wedding *[New tradition – shop for both outfits together or schedule a First Look photo opportunity before the ceremony]*

- the bride was kidnapped by fairies because she arrived on time *[New Tradition – forget being late, be respectful of your guests and plan to walk down the aisle on time]*

- the bride was possessed by evil spirits that entered her body because her feet touched the ground *[New Tradition: define the aisle any way you like]*

- future fertility was assured or compromised by the throwing of confetti, rice, etc or lack thereof. *[New Tradition: Anything that allows your guests to express their joie de vivre at your nuptials]*.

As a pregnant bride you are free to focus on the true significance of your wedding, and on your marriage, and let go of any compulsion to have, do, or include something just to ensure good luck or avoid bad luck because you have the best excuse of all to omit any fertility tradition that doesn't appeal to you.

11 HOW TO HAVE A STRESS-FREE WEDDING IN A PUBLIC PLACE

Outdoor ceremonies can provide the opportunity to further personalize your special day by holding it in a location that has some emotional significance for you, that provides a magnificent backdrop for your photographs, or where you will be able to take your child in the future.

However, there are a number of issues that you need to be aware of before you send out your invitations. While you can generally gather informally in most parks and on beaches, unless you make a booking you cannot guarantee that the area will be free. Starting your ceremony by frantically trying to find a place suitable for the ceremony is not conducive to a feeling of romance and satisfaction.

Permits, fees and conditions

- Contact the relevant local authority early to check on fees, conditions of use, and what permits are required.

- Some local authorities will charge you to book designated locations in a park, others may not. The norm seems to be a 2 hour booking which includes set-up and take-down time for your wedding decorator.

- If you are planning to use the services of a wedding decorator, or to provide chairs for guests to sit on, making a booking is highly advised.

- If you need power – for example to use an electronic keyboard – a booking is imperative in most parks.

- There may be prohibitions against recorded music, use of amplification, scattering of rose-petals, throwing of confetti, erection of shelters or wedding arches, tying anything to trees, and consumption of food and drink.

- There may be restrictions on where you may hold the gathering within a park or on a beach, and this may be related to the size of the gathering.

Arrival and introduction of guests

- Ensure that all guests know precisely where in the park/on the beach the ceremony is being held. Provide information about parking, how they get to the ceremony site from the car-park, and how long it will take them to walk the distance. It is also helpful to let them know what sort of terrain they will be walking across.

- If you are planning to make an entrance, delegate someone to meet and greet guests as they arrive. If there are to be a large number of guests, it may be appropriate to delegate this task to several people.

- Ensure that someone is delegated to introduce your officiant (celebrant) to guests who are mentioned or honored in the ceremony.

The Ceremony Space

People, public address systems, and musical instruments, particular wooden and string instruments all react badly to heat, direct sunshine, wind, and rain.

- Consider both hot and wet weather. There should be a suitable space either indoors or under cover in case bad weather prevents you holding the ceremony outside. And you should ensure that you and the guests are in shade.

- It is important that your guests are close enough to where you and your officiant will be located in order to form an intimate grouping and to ensure that everyone hears and sees the ceremony. The layout needs to be in place before the guests arrive.

- If you are planning to sign documents (marriage register or marriage license) as part of the ceremony, ensure that the table is big enough to comfortably hold them and anything else that will be used during the ceremony (candles, etc).

Health and Safety

- Ensure access to the ceremony space is safe and suitable for the elderly, anyone with mobility problems, and parents with prams.

- Ensure that any temporary shelter, such as a hired marquee, is well erected, properly secured, and safe.

- Water, cliffs, steps, and stairs are all potential hazards. Ensure that children are properly supervised at all times, and that elderly or infirm guests are given assistance where necessary.

- Severe sunburn can occur in a very short time, and heat and sun can cause dehydration, particularly at the hottest time of the day, so it is best to position everyone in the shade for a daytime ceremony. To prevent anyone becoming dehydrated think about providing water or other non-alcoholic liquid as guests arrive. This is particularly important for you because when you're pregnant you are especially at risk of suffering heatstroke which can be life-threatening for your baby.

12 HOW TO HAVE A STRESS-FREE BACKYARD WEDDING

There is no better way to ensure you have a stress-free day than to hold your wedding in your own home. Of course, there will be the stress of making sure that your house and garden are in tip-top condition for the day, but the benefit is that on the day you'll have only a short walk from your bedroom to the ceremony space, and therefore you'll be far more relaxed.

Arrival and introduction of guests

- If you are planning to make an entrance, delegate someone to meet and greet guests as they arrive. If there are to be a large number of guests, it may be appropriate to delegate this task to several people.

- Ensure that someone is delegated to introduce your officiant to guests who are mentioned or honored in the ceremony.

The Ceremony Space

- Consider both hot and inclement weather. There should be a suitable space either inside or under cover in case bad weather prevents holding the ceremony outside.

- It is important that your guests are close enough to where you and the officiant will be positioned in order to form an intimate grouping and to ensure that everyone hears and sees the ceremony. The layout needs to be in place before the guests arrive.

- If you are planning to sign documents as part of the ceremony (marriage register or marriage license) ensure that the table is big enough to comfortably hold them and anything else that will be used during the ceremony (candles, etc).

Noise

- Outside ceremonies are subject to all manner of external noise disturbances such as aircraft, animals, lawnmowers and so on. If your ceremony is scheduled to take place during the day you might consider asking your neighbors to refrain from using their lawnmowers or power tools for the period of the ceremony (allow a little leeway either side).

- If noise is likely to disturb the ceremony, it may be more appropriate to hold the ceremony indoors.

Number of Guests

- The maximum number of guests that can be accommodated to ensure a successful ceremony is dictated by the maximum number of people that will fit comfortably into the inside room or covered space.

Bathroom Facilities

- One toilet per 35 guests is the recommended ratio.

- If you don't have enough toilets to accommodate your guest numbers, consider hiring portapotties.

Children and Animals

- Small children can find it difficult to be quiet and listen to the ceremony. If there are to be large numbers of small children attending, you may find it useful to delegate someone to take care of them away from the ceremony space. Provision of play leaders or even a jumping castle has been very successful in my experience, but something as simple as a child-friendly DVD and a 'sitter' works well too.

- Any domestic animals that could interfere with the ceremony, or become unsettled by the guests, should be shut away or put in the kennels for the day.

Health and Safety
- Entrances and exits to the property and to the ceremony space should be clear and safe to use

- Constructions in gardens, whether temporary, such as hired marquees, or permanent, such as gazebos and rotundas, or garden art, should be well erected, properly secured and safe.

- Outside electrical equipment, for example sound equipment, must be safe. There should be no trailing leads, wires or cables. Leads and cables should be kept well away from walkway areas, and firmly taped down.

- Garden ponds and pools are a potential hazard for young children and thus access to them should be made safe.

- Severe sunburn can occur in a very short time, and heat and sun can cause dehydration, particularly at the hottest time of the day, so it is best to position everyone in the shade for a daytime ceremony. To guard against dehydration think about making sure everyone has water or other non-alcoholic liquid soon after they arrive.

Insurance
- Check that your domestic insurance policy covers third party liability for any visitors to the home.

13 HOW TO CREATE A MULTI-PURPOSE PLAN B

If you have chosen to have your wedding outdoors you will naturally hope that the weather will be perfect – nice and sunny but not too hot. But we can't control the weather so you should have a back-up plan that is as good as the primary plan.

Contingency plans (commonly called Plan B) take time to pull together, so the sooner you get started, the better. The further off your wedding is, the more options you will have.

The most popular choice for an alternative venue is usually either the reception venue or a shelter of some sort in the same vicinity of a planned outdoor wedding. Unfortunately an all-purpose approach may not be an adequate alternative on the day.

In particular, differing reasons for needing to activate your Plan B may well require differing solutions. An alternative venue suitable for heavy rain, for example, may not be available in case of forest fire or flooding, and you do need to have a plan B in place even if your Plan A venue is an indoor space or your ceremony and reception are being held in the same venue.

If your ceremony is to be at the same venue as the reception, or if your reception venue is your Plan B for your ceremony, you should ascertain the following:

- Will the space be available at the time you've planned for your ceremony to start? If your reception venue has an earlier booking on your day you may not be able to start your ceremony until after the previous function has concluded and the staff has had time to clean up and rearrange the space.

- Is the space adequate for the size of your bridal party and the number of guests for the ceremonial part of your day?

- Will your photographer be able to move around the space sufficiently to get good photos?

Read on for a range of issues you should consider and then work towards creating a written multipurpose Plan B (that is, one that incorporates plans B1, B2, B3, B4 and so on) in order to be ready for the full range of unwished-for possibilities.

Plan B1: In Case of Rain, Hail, and Storms

There is rain, and there is RAIN. Wet weather can mean anything from a drizzle to a downpour. Rain might be accompanied by hail, thunder, or lightning, or all three. When considering an alternative plan for your outdoor ceremony venue you need to take all of the following into account:

- How will the guests and the bridal party get to the venue from where they need to park?

- How likely is it that the car park, or the route from it, will be awash?

- How weather-proof is the alternative? A rotunda may work well in light rain, but driving rain will blow in under the roof, and guests and bridal party will be drenched before they reach it.

- Will the location be dangerous in a thunderstorm? Remember, being near or under a tree is extremely dangerous when there is lightning – and don't forget the possibility of dry lightning out of a clear sky when there are storms in the greater area.

- How audible will the ceremony in heavy rain? Many rotundas and shelters in parks have an unlined metal roof and the noise of rain or hail will drown out most public address systems.

Plan B2: In Case of High Winds

Wind is not only unpleasant, it is noisy, and a sunny day may also be extremely windy. Strong winds will turn furniture into missiles, play havoc with hair, veils, hats, and skirts. In addition, there is a not inconsiderable risk that legal paperwork, including your marriage license or marriage certificate, will take off, never to be seen again. Very high winds can bring trees down and severely damage or demolish built structures. High winds can also create dust storms.

Plan B3: In Case of Extreme Heat

Extreme heat is dangerous, particularly for your grandparents, small children, yourself and anyone else who is pregnant, or anyone with a health condition. Many outdoor venues have inadequate shade or no shade at all, and guests often have to walk some distance in the heat from where they park their cars, so, even if the ceremony starts on time the guests will have been outside in the heat for some considerable time.

A pop-up shelter is not a very satisfactory solution because it will exacerbate the heat unless it has very efficient vents to allow hot air to escape – which is almost never the case. And, of course, not only will a member of the bridal party or a guest collapsing bring your ceremony to a crashing halt, if the person who collapses is one of the couple getting married, the wedding may have to be postponed until a medical clearance is obtained.

An indoor venue may also become unbearably hot if it is not air-conditioned, or only has ceiling fans, or if ventilation is inadequate. This can be a significant problem in chapels or club rooms that remain closed until just before the ceremony start time.

B4: In Case of Flood

In a flood the venue may be inundated or access to it cut off. Is your Plan A venue in an area prone to flooding? Do you have an alternative that is not only above flood level, but where access will be unimpeded by flooding? Don't forget that flash-flooding can occur with little or no warning.

B5: In Case of Forest Fire or Total Fire Ban

When there is a high risk of fire or a fire is in progress, the following issues may prompt relocation of your wedding even though the venue is not under direct threat.

- Heavy smoke

- Extreme Heat

- Total Fire Ban making it illegal to have a planned Unity Candle ritual or a Memorial Candle honoring loved ones who have passed

B6: In Case of Non-Availability of your Plan A or your Reception Venue

In addition to weather-related events that may render your Plan A and/or Reception venue unfit for use, the venue may become unavailable for a number of localized reasons

- A fire in the building damages or destroys the venue

- Sewerage backup, leak, or overflow

- Water leaks from broken pipes or failed washers

- Venue was double-booked

- Business failure (venue closed by administrators)

It is really important that you read the terms of your contract carefully. Many venues spell out terms and conditions relating to you cancelling, but say little about what they will do should they be unable to fulfill their contract with you.

Do your best to get in writing what they will do for you should they be unable for fulfill the contract. At the very least you should obtain a guarantee that they will fully refund monies paid if they are unable to provide, at their expense, an alternate venue of equivalent or superior quality.

However, if a local weather event renders your venue unusable **do not cancel** as doing so may allow the venue to invoke their terms and conditions and refuse you a refund. Rather, contact the venue and ask what alternative arrangements do they have in place.

Give your Guests a Heads-Up

Give your guests full information about your plan A with your invitation and let them know that a Plan B is in place, what it is in case of wet weather, and how they will be notified.

A simple solution is to provide a phone number for them to call where they can listen to a recorded announcement but are not able to leave message. You will need someone you can rely on to lend you their phone number and create the required recorded message.

Design your Plan B Ceremony Space

Just because it is your backup plan doesn't make the ceremony space any less important. You will want to be happy with it if you have to implement it, so plan how you want your Plan B space to look.

- Where will the wedding party be located? Consult with your officiant as the way your bridal party is arranged has a huge impact on the success of the ceremony.

- Is seating available for you if you need it during the ceremony?

- Where will the signing table or table for items to be used in the ceremony be situated if one is needed?

- How will the chairs be arranged?

- Where will flowers or other ceremony decor be placed?

Activating the appropriate alternative plan

You need to plan how to activate the appropriate Plan B

- Who will make the decision that your Plan A is no longer viable? The designated person should not be the bride as the person needs, if necessary, to be free to carry out an on-site inspection in order to make an informed decision.

- What is the deadline by which the decision to move to the appropriate Plan B will be made?

- How will the change of plan be communicated?

- You will need to notify:

  - The alternative venue (should be told first as preparations may need to be done)

  - Your officiant (should be told next)

  - The person responsible for setting up the recorded announcement

  - Members of the bridal party

  - Your photographer

  - Your videographer

  - Your DJ or musicians

- Limo company (may need to collect you earlier than originally planned)

- Anyone making deliveries to the venue

- The guests if the reason for a change of venue is not one that will prompt them to call the designated number, for example, something very local to the venue.

Investigate Wedding Insurance

Wedding insurance may minimize the amount you lose in the event of being unable to hold your wedding because of local natural disaster or other unforeseen event.

Read the fine print to be sure you are clear what is covered and what is not. You may only be paid out in cases of cancellation. If your wedding or reception is relocated you are unlikely to be paid out.

14 HOW TO HAVE STRESS-FREE RELATIONSHIPS WITH SERVICE PROVIDERS

As the white wedding industry has developed, more and more specialist services and vendors have been added to the mix. It is not unusual for a couple to engage the services of 20, 30, or even 40 individual suppliers.

A common cause of stress is being let down at the last minute by vendors who cancel because they have overbooked, have realized that they are not up to the task, or have just decided they would rather do something else, such as go on vacation.

Another not uncommon cause of stress is discovering, after you've booked and paid a non-refundable deposit, that items or services you assumed were included are not, and if available, will incur a further charge.

The key to a stress-free relationship is to test all your assumptions before making a firm booking by asking questions about:

- what is included in the fee?

- how will the service be provided?

- who will actually provide the service on the day?

And then make sure that everything is fully documented in a formal contract.

It also is a good idea to touch base with your suppliers at regular intervals in the period between booking and your wedding day.

15 HOW TO MANAGE WHAT YOUR GUESTS SHARE ON SOCIAL MEDIA

Virtually everyone at your wedding is going to have the means to take photographs and to share them, together with comments they may feel like making about your wedding, with the world.

If that won't worry you, then it is not a problem. But if it will, if you have concerns about privacy, you can minimize the stress by having an unplugged or semi-unplugged wedding.

While you probably won't want to go to the lengths that some celebrities have – confiscating your guests' phones and tablets – you may wish to consider asking your guests to put their devices away, at least for the ceremony.

You could also ask them not to post pictures or comments to social media but instead to send you the photographs so you can post them at a later date, tagging everyone present at the wedding so they can also see them.

There are a number of ways to express your wishes:

- Include a heads-up that you are having an unplugged or semi-unplugged wedding with your invitation

- Include specific requests about what you wish your guests to do/not to do in your ceremony program

- Make sure your photographer and videographer understand your wishes and have agreed to abide by them - including not posting photographs or footage to social media sites or on their web pages. Get this in writing.

- Set up signs at the entrance to the ceremony space.

- Ask your officiant to make an announcement before you make your grand entrance.

16 HOW TO HAVE A STRESS-FREE START TO YOUR HONEYMOON

Organizing a wedding while pregnant can be exhausting, so plan a honeymoon that is relaxing, realistic in terms of budget and travel, and provides opportunities to indulge in some peace, quiet, and pampering.

Flying is usually not a problem until the final month as long as your pregnancy has been uncomplicated and your doctor approves. However, if you are planning to fly, you should check airline policies on pregnant passengers before making a booking. Many airlines have rules about how close to your due date you can fly. They may also require a medical certificate to prove you're not too close to your due date before they allow you to board the aircraft.

Make sure that your travel insurance covers pregnancy complications and premature births. Research hospitals at your destination so you know where they are. Carry a medical report and referral from your doctor in case you need to consult a physician while you're away.

If you are planning to change your name by marriage, don't forget that, due to heightened security, any booking you make with an airline must be in the same name as that on your ID documents, including your passport. If you are planning to fly soon after your wedding do not book your flights in your married name as it does take some weeks to obtain your official certificate or copy of your marriage license and then change your driver license, passport and other identity documentation over to your new name.

Some airlines will allow you to change the name on a ticket, depending on terms and conditions of your booking, but will charge you a considerable amount to do so. Others will make you buy a whole new ticket.

.

17 LAST WORDS OF ADVICE

Don't continue shopping

Continuing to 'shop' in order to confirm that you've made a good decision is a significant cause of stress. Once you've bought your dress, signed up your photographer, booked your venue, etc cross that task off your to-do list and move on.

Use Pinterest, Wedding Magazines and other pictorial sources as inspiration not a prescription.

Insisting that anything is exactly like the picture will add stress – it may not be practical or possible and it might not be affordable.

Don't let anyone relive their wedding vicariously through yours

Not your parents, not your friends, not any of your wedding suppliers. Don't waste time or effort trying to please everyone. It never works.

Don't forget to take breaks

Declare some days wedding free, where talking about the wedding is banned. Taking time off from the planning to have some fun together and to make plans and prepare for the baby will ensure you enjoy your big day.

Plan your marriage too

Our culture places a tremendous emphasis on having a great wedding and not enough on having an awesome marriage. It's okay to be temporarily obsessed and hanker after the perfect wedding -- but you have to keep your eye on what is truly important. Spend at least an equal amount of time planning for your marriage. Discuss every aspect of the life you hope to have together. Share any concerns you might have. Attend pre-marriage education if at all possible.

Accept that not everything will go according to plan

But if you don't let whatever it is put a dent in your day, you go with the flow and accept whatever happens with dignity and humour, you'll realize that it is the things that don't go according to plan that end up becoming your unique wedding memories - priceless because they weren't planned.

Take care of the legal requirements early

Don't leave applying for your marriage license or giving formal notice of your intention to marriage to the last minute. Check if you need official copies of identity or divorce documents and obtain them sooner rather than later.

ABOUT THE AUTHOR

Jennifer Cram is an award-winning professional marriage celebrant (wedding officiant) appointed by the Attorney General to officiate marriages in all states and territories of Australia. She is currently based in Brisbane, Queensland, where each year she creates and officiates in excess of one hundred ceremonies.

For many years her couples have voted her one of the top celebrants in the country and in 2013 she was named Queensland's top celebrant in the Australian Bridal Industry Academy Awards.

www.jennifercram.com.au
www.pride ceremonies.com.au